REAL OUTDOOR
SCIENCE EXPERIMENTS

REAL
Outdoor
Science
EXPERIMENTS

25+ Exciting STEAM Activities for Kids

Jenny Ballif

Photography by Evi Abeler

ROCKRIDGE
PRESS

First Rockridge Press trade paperback edition 2022

Rockridge Press and the Rockridge Press logo are trademarks or registered trademarks of Callisto Media Inc. and/or its affiliates in the United States and other countries and may not be used without written permission.

For general information on our other products and services, please contact our Customer Care Department within the United States at (866) 744-2665, or outside the United States at (510) 253-0500.

Paperback ISBN: 979-8-88608-777-2
eBook ISBN: 979-8-88650-195-7

Manufactured in the United States of America

Series Designer: Sean Doyle
Interior and Cover Designer: Brieanna H. Felschow
Art Producer: Samantha Ulban
Editor: Annie Choi
Production Editor: Ruth Sakata Corley
Production Manager: Martin Worthingtom

Photography © 2022 Evi Abeler.
Illustrations by Jenny Ballif, pp. 30, 42, 99
Author photo courtesy of Bob Bartholomew

10 9 8 7 6 5 4 3 2 1 0

To Mrs. Hudleson's second-grade class, who first started calling me Science Mom. We didn't know it then, but that nickname would change my life.

CONTENTS

INTRODUCTION

Welcome to *Real Outdoor Science Experiments*!

I'm Jenny Ballif, a scientist and an educator. Over the past decade, I've been sharing science demonstrations with kids around the world through virtual and in-person lessons.

Kids always ask me how I became a scientist. College and graduate school played an important role, but the best answer is mud pies.

When I was about seven years old, I created a recipe for the perfect mud pie. It was an artistic type of brick made of soil, water, and dried grass. Some people might say I was just playing in the dirt, but my search for the perfect mud pie involved several days of trial and error. I was inventing hypotheses and testing them, and when finished, I wrote down what I had learned! It really was the **scientific method** in action.

Years later, I went to college and studied agriculture and crop science. Then I went to graduate school to study plant science and molecular biology, which studies how molecules interact with one another in living organisms. I learned great things in graduate school, but it was the curiosity, wonder, and dedication learned in childhood that shaped me the most as a scientist.

You might think of science as something you can do only with fancy degrees and credentials. But you can start using your curiosity and critical thinking right now! Getting outside and exploring what's around you are great ways to start thinking like a scientist.

In this book, you'll find 29 of my favorite outdoor science experiments. Completing these experiments will teach you new and useful skills, like how to make rope or ink from plants, and help you understand the world around you. You'll also explore questions that relate to everyday life. How do seeds know when to sprout? Why do people put salt on roads in winter? What do snails eat? In this book, you'll find the answers to these questions and more!

Chapter One

Science and the Outdoors

What is the outdoors? Put simply, it is any open area outside your home. Even if you spend most of your time indoors, you are still connected to the outside world.

The wood and metal used to make your home or school building came from forests and rock. Your food comes from farms, oceans, or rivers. In fact, almost *everything* inside comes from something that was once outside.

But nature gives you more than just building materials. Rock and water cycle from one form to another, providing drinking water, the weather you experience, and the **energy** and minerals that power your home. Each part of the outdoors is connected to how you live!

One of the best ways to explore the outdoors is with "STEAM," which stands for science, technology, engineering, art, and mathematics. These fields of study will help you better understand the natural world.

SCIENCE

The word *science* comes from the Latin word *scientia*, which means "knowledge." But science is more than just knowledge. It's also a process that helps you understand the world, with testable explanations and predictions! There are many branches of science, and many connect to the outdoors.

The weather you experience each day is physics in action. Have you ever wondered how sunscreen works or why strawberries turn red when they ripen? Chemistry has the answers! Biology explains how birds know where to migrate, and geology can predict where earthquakes or sinkholes will occur. These are just a few examples of how each branch of science uses careful observations, predictions, and evaluations to help us understand the natural world.

TECHNOLOGY

You might think of the outdoors as being the opposite of technology, but nature has inspired many inventions!

In the 1940s, a Swiss scientist out for a walk noticed how the seeds of a burdock plant stuck to his clothes—and his dog. These burrs had lots of small hooks. By imitating this design, George de Mestral invented Velcro, the original hook-and-loop fastener.

Papermaking was inspired by wasps that chew wood into pulp and mix it with their saliva to form paper nests. The earliest recipes for paper are thousands of years old!

Some of today's most useful computer programs are based on the movement of ants. These "ant colony optimization" programs show truck drivers the most efficient routes to travel, improve how cell phones and computers work, and help scientists understand life in the cell.

ENGINEERING

Engineering is all about building things. Human engineers build engines, machines, and structures, like buildings or bridges. By modeling designs after nature, people are often able to build better things!

In Japan, bullet trains traveled so fast they created shock waves as they went through tunnels. The loud noise disturbed people and damaged the tunnels, too. How did they fix the problem? Kingfishers! The kingfisher bird is able to dive into water with hardly any splash, so Japanese engineers reshaped the front of the bullet train to be like a kingfisher's beak. The new trains were 10 percent faster, used 15 percent less electricity, and went in and out of tunnels without the booming shock waves.

Humpback whales have unusual fins with bumps called tubercles. Scientists realized that the tubercles reduced drag and improved lift. They applied a similar design to wind turbines, and the newly designed turbines generated more power. These are just two examples of how **biomimicry** has improved human machines and tools.

ART

From sunsets and flowers to birdsongs and mountains, the outdoors is full of beauty! Nature has inspired artists since the first cave paintings more than 40,000 years ago and continues to be a source of creativity and innovation today.

Art helps people better understand nature, too. Early scientists such as Alexander von Humboldt drew sketches of the animals and plants they observed. Try it! Creating art can help you notice more details and appreciate the natural world even more.

MATH

Math is more than counting. It's also used to describe and predict patterns and to study **symmetry**.

Geometry can measure ripples in a pond or predict the height of tsunami waves. Linear algebra allows people to convert data from satellites into pictures and maps. And mathematical models are used to predict thunderstorms and hurricanes.

The repeating shapes of a fern leaf, tree branches, and snowflakes follow a mathematical pattern called a fractal. Snail shells, hurricanes, and spiral galaxies all conform to a mathematical relationship called the golden ratio.

The natural world is full of patterns and symmetry that can be modeled using math! The more time you spend outdoors, the more math connections you'll discover.

SCIENTIFIC METHOD

In each area of STEAM, people find questions that need to be answered. A biologist might be trying to understand why a group of penguins is laying fewer eggs, or a game designer may need a new line of code to make their virtual world work. No matter what question people have, one of the best ways to find answers is using the scientific method.

Let's say you accidentally dropped Mentos candy into your soda bottle, and the soda erupted out of the bottle. You might wonder why this happened and look up explanations online. Several say it's because of a chemical reaction, where the sugar in the candy reacts to make bubbles of gas. But other sources say it's due to the rough texture of the Mentos candies, which provides a surface for bubbles to form on. These are two very different possible explanations. In the first, the gas comes from a chemical reaction. In the second, the gas is already inside the carbonated soda.

How could you find out which explanation is correct? By forming a **hypothesis** and testing it! A hypothesis is an explanation that can be tested. Let's look at how you could test each explanation in the Mentos-and-soda example:

If the sugar in the Mentos reacts with the soda to form bubbles, then sugar in other candy, like gummy bears, should do the same thing. But when you drop a gummy bear into the soda bottle, nothing happens, proving this hypothesis is incorrect. Sugar alone isn't the cause.

If Mentos' rough texture is the reason, then something else with a similar texture, like sand, should produce the same effect. You then put sand in the soda and it creates even more

bubbles than the Mentos did. Mystery solved! The results of your experiment prove it's the texture of the Mentos, not their sugar, that causes the bubbling reaction.

We'll use the scientific method in this book to learn more about the outdoors. Each activity includes directions to help you:

- Explore a question
- Form a hypothesis
- Test the hypothesis
- Collect and analyze data
- Draw conclusions about the hypothesis
- Consider future research

As you follow along, these steps will teach you more about the natural world and how to discover new things. In the next chapter, I'll show you how to use this book so you get the full benefits of using the scientific method in each activity.

Chapter Two

How to Use This Book

The activities in this book are divided into four chapters, each covering a topic connected to the outdoors. Within each chapter, the experiments are arranged from easier to more challenging. You don't have to do them in order—it's perfectly fine to jump around from section to section.

If you're interested in exploring nature, start with chapter 3, where you can learn how to create the perfect snail habitat and understand seeds and leaves. If creating and using tools is your jam, try chapter 4, where you'll learn how to cook with the power of the sun and how to make rope from plants! To learn all about energy, go to chapter 5, which offers physics activities involving splatter paintings and rockets, and beautiful art made with a pendulum. Finally, chapter 6 explores **matter** and **elements** with chemistry experiments, like extracting **pigments** from leaves and making your own ink!

GETTING READY

Look through the experiments and see what sparks your interest!

Before choosing an experiment or activity, check the estimated time it will take and whether there are any safety cautions. If the weather isn't right, or if you don't have the needed materials, bookmark the activity for later. Some of the more advanced activities require adult supervision. Make sure you have a grown-up with you when attempting one of those!

Next, gather the needed materials. Many of the materials can be found outside, but, depending on the activity, you may also need to use things such as chalk, a jar or other container from the recycle bin, pencil and paper, scissors, string, or tape.

DOING THE EXPERIMENTS

When you have gathered your supplies and are ready to begin, read through the "Real Question" listed at the beginning of each activity to learn what the experiment is about and make your hypothesis.

If you don't know how to make a hypothesis, it helps to answer the question with an "if-then" statement. For example, let's say the question is "Will leaves in the shade be bigger or smaller than leaves in the sun?" Your if-then statement could be "*If* leaves are in shade, *then* they will be smaller because they don't get as much light." Or your statement could be "*If* leaves are in shade, *then* they will be bigger so they can capture more light."

Remember, a hypothesis is not a random guess. Your "then" statement is based on knowledge you have. A good hypothesis makes a prediction and connects two or more things that can change, which are called **variables**. Each activity is set up so it can be a full experiment, with one variable that changes and another that is measured. For example, in Be-leaf-able Shapes (page 12), the amount of sunlight the leaves have is the variable that changes. The size of the leaves is the variable that is measured.

When you are ready to start an activity, read through all the instructions before you begin. Then follow the step-by-step instructions in order.

The "Why?" section explains more about the background and process of each experiment. When you answer the questions in the "Observations" section, you see what the experiment revealed about your hypothesis.

The "STEAM Connection" will show you how the activity relates to other areas of science, technology, engineering, art, or math.

If you enjoyed what you explored, "Try This!" has ideas for how to expand the experiment into a new activity.

Remember, you can use the Glossary (page 104) to look up unfamiliar words, and it's okay if an experiment doesn't work out as expected! As every good scientist knows, mistakes are part of learning. What you learn is more important than the results, and sometimes failed experiments teach us the most!

Chapter Three

Experimenting with Nature

In this chapter, you will use science to dive into the amazing processes and inner workings of nature. These fun experiments will help you learn about biology, entomology (the study of insects), geology, and more. Along the way, you'll see that birds are smarter than you think, and snails are more than just slowpokes. With the help of some sugar, you will explore how sinkholes work. You will even make your own soil using worms. Ready to dive in?

BE-LEAF-ABLE SHAPES

LEVEL: EASY

TIME: 15 MINUTES

REAL QUESTION

Will leaves in the shade be bigger or smaller than leaves in sunny locations? Will shade leaves have different shapes than sun leaves?

⚠️ CAUTION: Do not pick leaves from poison ivy, poison oak, or poison sumac. If you don't know how to recognize these plants, refer to the Resources section (page 107).

MATERIALS

- leaves
- paper
- pencil

STEPS

1. Collect leaves from at least 5 different types of plants.

2. For each plant, try to find some leaves completely in the shade and others in full sun. Look for leaves on the top or outer part of a plant that are getting sunlight.

3. Then look for leaves near the trunk or ground that are in the shade.

4. On the paper, use the pencil to draw a chart comparing the size of the leaves for each plant. Record which leaf (the one in sunlight or the one in shade) is bigger for each plant.

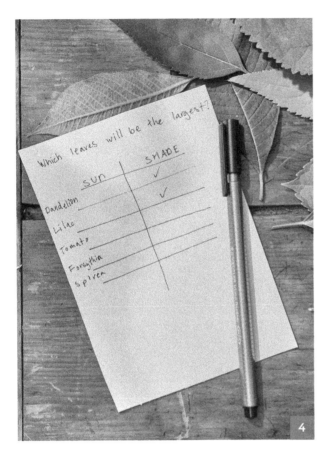

Which leaves will be the largest?

	SHADE
sun	✓
Dandelion	✓
Lilac	
Tomato	
Forsythia	
Spirea	

4

5. Look at your chart and evaluate your results. On average, which leaves are bigger: the shade leaves or the sun leaves?

WHY? To perform **photosynthesis**, leaves use **chlorophyll** to absorb light. The larger the leaf, the more light it can absorb. But larger leaves also lose more water from small pores called **stomata**. A plant can't afford to lose too much water! This is why leaves in full sun are often smaller and lighter in color than leaves in shade. Leaves in shade often need more chlorophyll to harvest light, which gives them a darker color.

STEAM Connection: Like leaves, solar panels use sunlight as a power source. The shape and size of each panel make a big difference in how much electricity it can produce.

OBSERVATIONS: Did you find any plants that grow only in shady areas? What size and shape were their leaves?

Try This! Compare the leaves in aquatic (water) and terrestrial (land) plants. What similarities or differences do you notice between the plants' leaf colors, shapes, stems, and roots?

SUGAR SINKHOLES

LEVEL: EASY

TIME: 20 MINUTES

REAL QUESTION

A sinkhole—some of which are big enough to swallow entire buildings!—is a naturally occurring depression or hole in the ground. How do sinkholes form?

MATERIALS

- cardboard tube, such as an empty paper towel roll
- empty flowerpot or container with drainage holes in the bottom
- 2 cups gravel or pebbles
- 1 to 2 cups sugar
- dirt (enough to fill the flowerpot)
- water
- large container, with no holes, big enough to hold the flowerpot

STEPS

1. Place the tube upright in the center of the flowerpot.

2. Add the gravel around the bottom of the tube to stabilize it. Then pour the sugar into the tube.

3. Place dirt on top of the gravel until the dirt is even with the top of the sugar.

CONTINUED ➡

4. Slowly remove the tube by pulling it straight up. You should see a white circle of sugar in the center of the dirt.

5. Spread a thin layer of dirt over everything in the flowerpot.

6. To simulate groundwater, add a few inches of water to the larger container. Place the flowerpot in the container so the bottom of the pot is submerged in the water.

7. Observe what happens to the dirt and sugar as water enters the flowerpot from the drainage holes below.

WHY? Rocks such as granite or sandstone (represented by the gravel) do not dissolve in rainwater, but limestone (represented by the sugar) does! When limestone dissolves, or is eroded away from soil, caves and underground caverns can form as a result. A sinkhole forms when the ground on top of a cave collapses.

STEAM Connection: Scientists use radar technology to discover where sinkholes are forming. Because radio and sound waves travel differently through different materials, scientists can use these waves to see underground chambers and predict a sinkhole before the collapse happens!

OBSERVATIONS: Did the sugar sinkhole form faster or slower than you expected?

Try This! Instead of letting water seep in from below, sprinkle some on top to simulate rain.

SUPER SNAILS

TIME: 20 MINUTES TO SET UP,
PLUS 3 DAYS TO OBSERVE

REAL QUESTION

Where do snails and slugs live? What do they eat?

! CAUTION: After observing your snails, return them to the same place you found them. Never release a snail from a pet store outside.

MATERIALS

- empty clear container
- dirt
- brown material, such as dead leaves and twigs
- green material, such as moss and fresh leaves
- water
- 4 snails or slugs (found outside)
- plastic wrap or a clear lid with holes in it

STEPS

1. Use the container to gather materials for your snail habitat.

2. Cover the bottom of the container with dirt. Cover half the dirt with brown material, such as dead leaves and twigs.

3. Cover the other half with green material, such as moss and fresh leaves. Add enough water to the container to make everything damp.

4. Find 4 or more snails or slugs. Look in damp areas, such as under bushes or leaf litter, or near leaves that have circular holes in them.

5. Place the snails or slugs into your habitat. Cover the container with the plastic wrap or lid. Be sure the cover has holes so the snails can breathe.

5

6. If the snails or slugs aren't active when you first place them in the habitat, check again in 30 minutes or so. Observe them for a few minutes or up to a few days.

WHY? Snails and slugs have a flexible mouth with tiny teeth, called a radula. They use their lower tentacles to taste and smell their environment. Their slime helps them move and climb. Detritivore snails eat dead or decaying material and prefer the brown side of the container. Herbivore snails prefer the green side.

STEAM Connection: Many snails live in rivers and the ocean. If the water's **pH** changes because of pollution or increased carbon dioxide, the snails' shells will look different. By observing snail shells, scientists can answer questions about the environment.

OBSERVATIONS: How did the snails or slugs move and eat? Did they breathe, poop, or hide?

Try This! Draw a picture of a snail or slug, imagining it has superpowers! Use your creativity to draw this amazing animal.

ROOTS OR SHOOTS?

LEVEL: MEDIUM

TIME: 20 MINUTES TO SET UP,
PLUS 3 WEEKS TO OBSERVE

REAL QUESTION

When seeds **germinate**, what comes first: the root or the shoot?

MATERIALS

- **3 types of seeds**
- **scissors**
- **3 paper cups or other small disposable container**
- **dirt**
- **water**
- **leaves or grass clippings**

STEPS

1. Find 3 different types of seeds from plants growing outside.

2. Carefully use the scissors to make small drainage holes in the bottom of each of the paper cups.

3. Fill the paper cups with dirt and add water until the dirt is damp.

4. Place one of each seed in a cup so they are half buried in the damp soil.

5. Place leaves or grass clippings over the seeds to help them stay damp.

6. During the next 3 weeks, check the seeds periodically to see if either roots or shoots are starting to emerge.

7. Add water when needed to keep the soil damp.

WHY? All plants, except moss and ferns, reproduce with seeds. A seed has a covering to protect it, and inside the seed is starch (food) and an embryo that will grow into the roots and shoots. Roots emerge first to find water and nutrients for the growing plant.

STEAM Connection: Every year, farmers plant seeds, but not all of them germinate. How do they know how to best space their seeds in the ground? Math! They use the germination rate to calculate how close together their seeds should be planted. That way, they don't end up with a field that is too crowded or too sparse.

OBSERVATIONS: What emerged first: the root or the shoot?

Try This! Some seeds germinate better when exposed to cold temperatures. Try placing seeds in the refrigerator for a few weeks and retesting the experiment. Does this help the seeds sprout?

BIRD BRAINS

LEVEL: MEDIUM

TIME: 20 MINUTES TO MAKE,
PLUS 3 TO 7 DAYS TO OBSERVE

REAL QUESTION

Are birds smart enough to uncover the treat?

⚠ CAUTIONS: Adult supervision is recommended when using a knife in this activity.

MATERIALS

- 1 orange or 2 paper cups
- knife
- spoon
- toothpick
- 4 (3-foot-long) pieces of yarn or string
- birdseed (black sunflower seeds will attract the widest variety of birds)
- napkin

STEPS

1. Carefully halve the orange with a knife. Use a spoon to scoop out the fruit, creating 2 orange rind bowls. Enjoy the orange fruit as a snack!

2. Use a toothpick to poke 4 holes into one orange rind bowl so that lines drawn between the holes would form an *X*.

CONTINUED ➜

3. Take 2 pieces of yarn. Use the toothpick to push 1 piece of yarn through two diagonally opposite holes. Push the other piece of yarn through the other two holes. When finished, the strings should form an *X* inside the bowl.

4. Repeat steps 2 and 3 with the other bowl. You should have 2 bowls each with an *X* shape made of string in the center.

5. Fill both bowls with birdseed. Cover one with a napkin, tucking the edges into the seed.

6. Tie the ends of the strings of each bowl together, and hang the bird feeders where you can observe them.

WHY? Birds have different levels of intelligence. Crows and jays are among the most intelligent bird species. If these birds visit your feeders, they'll almost certainly uncover the treats.

STEAM Connection: **The Puy du Fou theme park in France has six trained rooks that pick up litter in the park. Each time they place a piece of garbage in the trash-can, a small box opens and reveals a treat for the bird to eat.**

OBSERVATIONS: What types of birds did you observe at your feeder? Did any birds figure out the napkin trick and uncover the food?

Try This! Can birds pass a float test? If a treat is floating in water in a clear plastic pipe but can't be reached, dropping pebbles into the pipe raises the water level, bringing the treat within reach. Crows almost always pass this test.

DEDICATED DECOMPOSERS

LEVEL: MEDIUM

TIME: 20 MINUTES TO SET UP, PLUS 3 DAYS TO OBSERVE

REAL QUESTION

What do worms eat? How do worms make soil or **compost**?

MATERIALS

- transparent food storage container
- dirt
- water, if needed
- 3 to 5 worms
- 1 to 2 cups shredded paper, moistened with water
- 1 to 2 cups vegetable scraps, such as carrot peels, finely chopped
- cheesecloth or paper towel
- rubber band or string
- paper bag or cloth

STEPS

1. Fill the transparent container with dirt until it is halfway full. If the dirt is dry, add water until damp. Smooth the surface of the dirt but do not pack it down.

2. Place the worms on top of the dirt.

3. Cover half of the dirt with damp shredded paper. Cover the other half with vegetable scraps. These layers should be 1 to 2 inches deep.

WHY? Paper and vegetables are both **organic matter**. The paper is rich in carbon, and the vegetable scraps are rich in nitrogen. Worms eat organic matter and like a mixture of both carbon-rich and nitrogen-rich foods. Their diet and movement through soil play an important role in **decomposition**. As they eat decaying material, they convert it into compost that is beneficial to growing plants.

STEAM Connection: Mary Appelhof created an indoor composting bin in her basement filled with food scraps, bedding, and red wiggler worms. During the winter of 1972, the worms ate 65 pounds of garbage and created nutrient-rich compost for her garden.

4. Soak the cheesecloth or paper towel in water, then place it over the container. Secure it with a rubber band or string.

5. Cover the container with the paper bag or cloth so the environment is dark. Store the container indoors away from direct sunlight. Add water as needed to keep the dirt moist but not wet.

6. Over 3 days, observe the worms once a day by examining the sides of the container. Carefully move the paper and food scraps to observe the surface of the dirt. Do you see worm poop or tunnels? Can you tell what the worms have been eating?

OBSERVATIONS: In which half of the container did the worms spend most of their time?

Try This! Build a simple worm compost or **vermicompost** container by adding ventilation holes to the container. Place a tray below to collect excess liquid.

FISHING FOR INVERTEBRATES

LEVEL: CHALLENGING

TIME: 20 MINUTES

REAL QUESTION

What types of **invertebrates** live in a stream or river?

! CAUTION: It is dangerous to wade in rivers with fast currents. This activity is best suited for a smaller, shallow stream and done with adult supervision. Never attempt during flood conditions.

MATERIALS

- river or stream
- pie dish or other shallow container to hold water
- 2 (2-foot-long) sticks
- 1 (2-foot-long) piece of cheesecloth
- shoes that can get wet

STEPS

1. With an adult helper, locate a shallow river or stream. Be sure the water is safe to enter, and enter only with adult supervision.

2. Fill the pie dish with water. Set the dish aside at the bank of the river.

3. Next, tie two corners of the cheesecloth to the ends of 1 stick. Complete your net by tying the other two corners of the cheesecloth to the other stick.

CONTINUED →

4. Carefully walk into the river and slowly place one of the sticks flat on the bottom of the riverbed. Secure it with your feet, and hold the other stick at the water's surface. The current should give the cheesecloth net a scooped shape.

5. Have another person stand 6 to 10 feet upstream in the river. They should walk toward the cheesecloth net, moving their feet from side to side to turn over the rocks as they approach.

6. Pick up the cheesecloth net and empty the contents into the pie dish.

7. Observe the invertebrates caught by the net. After observing, release them back into the river.

WHY? Kicking rocks disturbs the invertebrates living in the river and the water's current carries them downstream. The cheesecloth net allows water to pass through but traps the invertebrates. Depending on where you are, you may see dragonfly nymphs, mayfly larvae (which have three tails), caddisflies, freshwater shrimp, leeches, or wigglers (mosquito larvae)!

STEAM Connection: Scientists can tell a lot about a river's water quality by studying the insect larvae that live there. Sampling invertebrates is an important part of the monitoring process.

OBSERVATIONS: How many different types of invertebrates did you observe?

Try This! Keep a journal of the invertebrates you find, drawing a picture of each. Try to find 10 different types of water animals.

Chapter Four

Experimenting with Structure and Tools

When you think of a tool, you probably imagine a screwdriver or wrench or something else made of metal and plastic. But there are many tools you can make yourself with items found outdoors! In this chapter, you will learn to make rope from plants, ink from berries, bricks from mud, and how to determine direction with the sun. Along the way, you'll explore concepts scientists use in fields like astronomy and engineering. You'll also learn more about the natural sources of common building materials.

SIDEWALK CHALK COMPASS

LEVEL: EASY

TIME: 10 MINUTES TO DRAW, PLUS 1 DAY TO OBSERVE

REAL QUESTION

Can you find north and south using shadows?

MATERIALS

- sidewalk, driveway, or other surface that can be drawn on with chalk
- sidewalk chalk
- tall object or person to cast a shadow
- timer or watch

STEPS

1. On a sunny day, find a flat surface, such as a sidewalk or driveway.

2. Using the chalk, mark the location of the object that will cast the shadow.

3. Make your first observation shortly after sunrise. Trace the object's shadow with the chalk. Then set the timer for 1 hour. When the timer goes off, return and trace the shadow again, making sure the object is in the same place. Use different colors each time to create an artistic pattern or a rainbow.

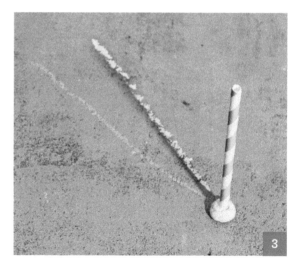

4. Continue tracing the shadow each hour until just before sunset.

5. After tracing the last shadow, draw a line connecting the endpoints of all of the shadows. This line is called a **gnomon curve**.

6. Find the point on the gnomon curve that is closest to the object that made the shadow. Draw a straight line from that point to the object. This line points directly north and south. You just made a solar compass!

WHY? As Earth rotates, the part that faces the sun changes. Shadows are longest in the morning and evening when the sun appears near the horizon. Because Earth rotates from west to east, the shortest shadows will point directly north or south.

STEAM Connection: The Greek philosopher Eratosthenes used changing shadows to prove Earth is round! He noticed that the amount of light entering a well was different depending on where the well had been dug.

OBSERVATIONS: Which shadows are the longest on your sidewalk chalk compass? Which shadows are shortest?

Try This! Use the same object to make a sundial at different times of the year! If possible, trace the same spot during the fall and spring **equinoxes** and winter and summer **solstices**.

BERRY GOOD INK

LEVEL: MEDIUM

TIME: 30 MINUTES

REAL QUESTION

What ink colors can be produced from natural materials, such as blackberries?

⚠ **CAUTION:** Do not make ink from poisonous plants. Do not ever eat ink.

MATERIALS

- **2 bowls**
- **1 cup fresh blackberries or other fresh berries**
- **fork**
- **cheesecloth or old piece of fabric**
- **1 teaspoon salt**
- **3 small cups or containers**
- **¼ teaspoon vinegar**
- **¼ teaspoon baking soda**
- **3 paintbrushes or sticks**
- **paper**

STEPS

1. In 1 bowl, mash the blackberries with the fork.

2. Place the cheesecloth over the second bowl.

3. Put the mashed berries on the cheesecloth and gather the corners. Squeeze gently over the bowl to collect the juice. Discard the seeds and pulp.

4. Add the salt to the juice and stir. Then divide the salt and juice mixture evenly among the 3 cups.

5. Add the vinegar to the first cup, add the baking soda to the second cup, and leave the third cup as is. Use the paintbrushes or sticks to stir each mixture.

6. Use each paintbrush or stick to draw or write with the blackberry ink on the paper.

WHY? Many berries and plants contain compounds called **anthocyanins**. Most of these pigments turn pink when they become more **acidic** (such as when exposed to vinegar) and turn blue when they become basic (such as when exposed to baking soda). The acidity can also affect how the pigments appear over time. Keep an eye on your paper. You might see another color change in a few days!

STEAM Connection: Some of the earliest known pigments were made from materials such as soot, earth, and chalk. During the Renaissance, Italians made the color ultramarine from the semiprecious stone lapis lazuli. It was the most expensive pigment in the world!

OBSERVATIONS: Did adding vinegar or baking soda change the color of the ink?

Try This! Make different colors of ink using avocado pits, walnuts, rose petals, or sunflower petals. Then make a feather quill by using a knife to trim the base of a feather to a point. Use the quill to write or draw with the ink you made.

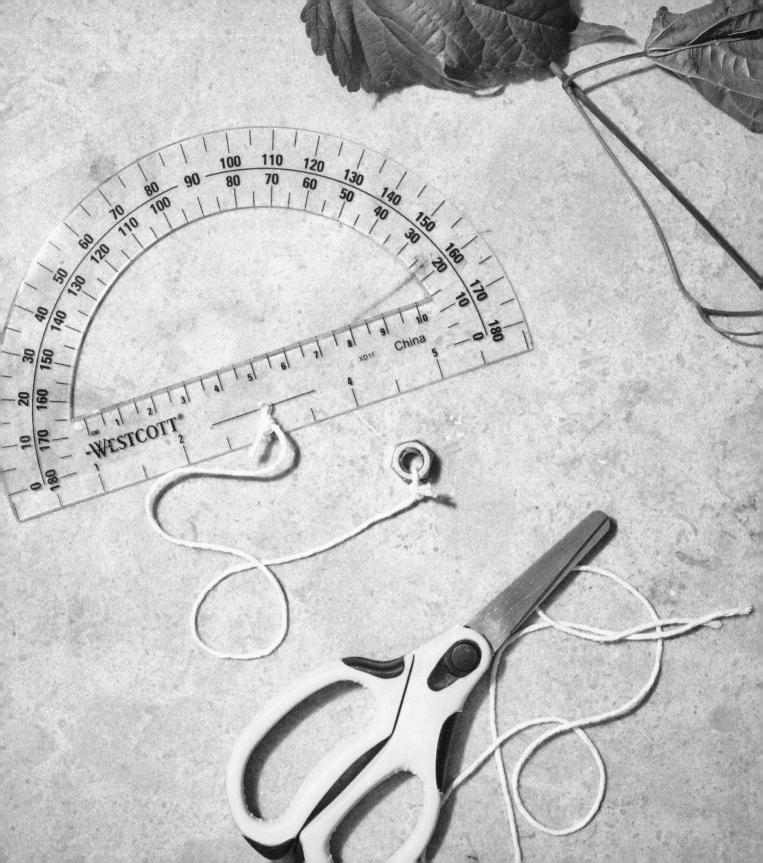

DIY INCLINOMETER

LEVEL: MEDIUM

TIME: 10 MINUTES TO MAKE,
PLUS 10 MINUTES TO OBSERVE

REAL QUESTION

Can you calculate your **latitude** by looking at the stars?

MATERIALS

- small weight, such as a pebble or washer
- 1 (1-foot-long) piece of thread
- protractor with a hole in the middle of its straight edge
- tape
- straw or a piece of paper rolled into a tube

STEPS

1. Tie the weight to one end of the thread. Push the other end of the thread through the hole in the protractor. Tie the thread onto the protractor so the weight hangs down several inches.

2. Tape the straw along the straight edge of the protractor, which is the top of your inclinometer.

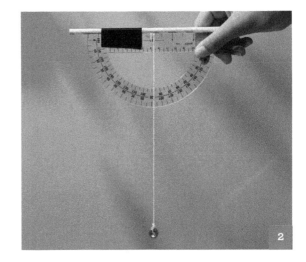

3. Take your inclinometer outside on a clear night.

   - If you're in the northern hemisphere, locate the North Star (Polaris): First, find the Big Dipper. The two stars at the end of the dipper's "cup" point to the North Star.

CONTINUED →

- If you're in the southern hemisphere, look for the Southern Cross. The two bright stars to the left of the cross are the pointer stars. Lines drawn from those toward the horizon intersect at Polaris Australis, a faint star that aligns with the South Pole.

4. Look through the straw and aim your inclinometer at Polaris or Polaris Australis. Press your finger against the bottom of the inclinometer where the string is. Note the degree mark that the string is touching and subtract that number from 90 (or subtract 90 from it if the number is bigger than 90). This is your latitude!

WHY? The North Star appears to remain at a fixed point because it is directly above the North Pole. The angle at which you view this star matches your latitude. Someone standing at the North Pole would have to look directly upward (90 degrees), whereas someone at the equator would have to look to the horizon (0 degrees), to view it.

STEAM Connection: Avalanche scientists use inclinometers to measure the slope of mountainsides. Because avalanches typically occur at slopes between 30 and 45 degrees, knowing the slope angle can save lives.

OBSERVATIONS: Were you able to find your latitude?

Try This! Repeat the exercise one or two hours after your first observation. What is different about the night sky now? What is the same?

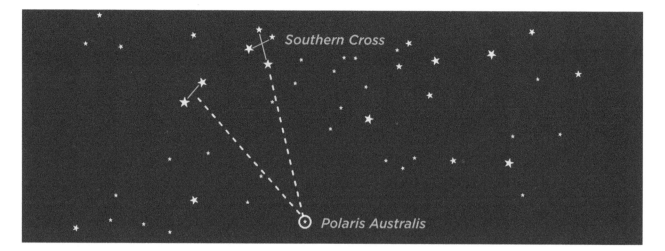

Southern Cross

Polaris Australis

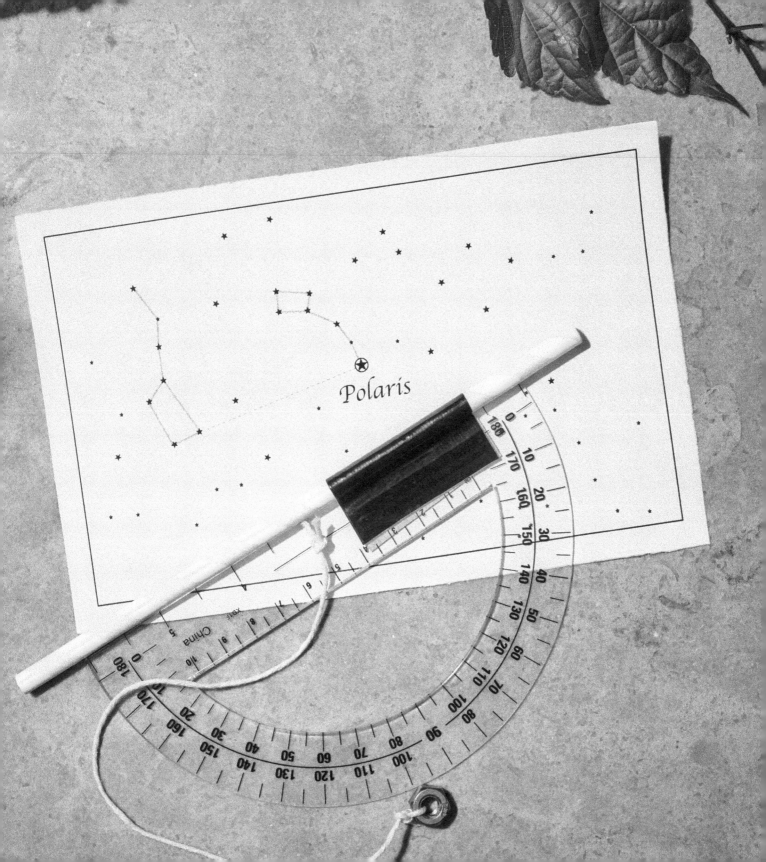

Polaris

MUD PIE CHALLENGE

LEVEL: MEDIUM

TIME: 15 MINUTES TO MAKE,
PLUS 1 TO 3 DAYS TO DRY

REAL QUESTION

What type of materials will make the most unbreakable mud pie?

MATERIALS

- **2 aluminum pie pans**
- **dirt**
- **water**
- **grass, straw, or crushed-up leaves (optional)**
- **stick**

STEPS

1. Fill each pie pan about three-fourths full of dirt.

2. Pour just enough water into each pan so the dirt is fully hydrated and becomes thick like peanut butter. Drain off excess water as needed. If desired, add a handful of grass, straw, or leaves.

3. Use the stick to stir one of the pans vigorously for 2 to 3 minutes. Do not stir the other pan.

4. Set both pans in a sunny location and let them dry completely. This may take 1 to 3 days.

5. Once the mud pies are dry, tip them upside down and carefully remove them from the pans.

CONTINUED →

WHY? Dirt is made of particles of different sizes. Sand has the largest particles and provides stability and structure. Clay is the smallest and binds soil together. You need both sand and clay to make a good mud pie. **Fibrous** material, like straw or hair, helps the mud pie dry more evenly and helps control shrinking or cracking. The stirring helps bind the clay particles to the rest of the material.

STEAM Connection: People have used mud to create bricks for thousands of years! Some of the oldest buildings on the planet are made from adobe, cob, or rammed earth. Today, bricks are still used in modern construction. They are fired or baked in an oven to make them even more **durable**.

OBSERVATIONS: Is the stirred mud pie stronger than the mud pie that was not stirred? How well do the different mud pies hold together under stress?

Try This! Use your best mud pie recipe to make a sculpture, vase, or brick wall!

SOLAR OVEN

LEVEL: MEDIUM

TIME: 30 MINUTES TO MAKE,
PLUS 2 HOURS TO COOK

REAL QUESTION

Can heat from light be captured or increased?

! CAUTION: Solar ovens get very hot.
Use oven mitts when checking
the oven. Have an adult help you
with this experiment.

MATERIALS

- **2 glass jars with lids**
- **black duct tape or black paint**
- **white duct tape or white paint**
- **hammer**
- **nail**
- **2 marshmallows or pieces of cheese**
- **2 oven bags**
- **oven mitts or a cloth**

STEPS

1. Cover the outside of 1 jar and its lid with
    black duct tape or paint so it is completely
    black. Use white tape or paint to cover the
    other jar and its lid and make it white.

2. With an adult helper, use the hammer and
    nail to carefully poke a hole through the lid of
    each jar.

3. Place 1 marshmallow or piece of cheese in each jar. Put the lid on and seal the jar.

4. On a sunny day, place each jar in an oven bag. Blow air into the bag so there is space all around the jar. Tie the end of the bag into a knot to keep the air inside the bag. Your solar ovens are ready to cook! Place them outside in full sun.

5. After 2 hours, check on your ovens. Use the oven mitts to open the jars.

6. Observe the marshmallows or cheeses.

WHY? Lighter surfaces have a high **albedo**, meaning most of the light energy that hits them is reflected back into the atmosphere. Dark surfaces have a low albedo and absorb most of the light energy, generating heat. This is why a black-colored surface becomes much hotter than a white one.

STEAM Connection: Some solar farms use reflected light to generate electricity. Mirrors aim light at a black tower, which becomes hot enough to boil water into steam, generating thousands of megawatts of electricity each year.

OBSERVATIONS: Which jar was hotter?

Try This! Increase the temperature of your solar oven by placing a reflector made of aluminum foil–covered cardboard around it.

WALL SMASH!

LEVEL: CHALLENGING

TIME: 30 MINUTES

REAL QUESTION

What material makes the strongest wall? What types of walls are strongest?

MATERIALS

- **tree branch or other structure to hang a rope from**
- **small and large rocks**
- **rope, yarn, or twine**
- **safety glasses or sunglasses**
- **stick**
- **dirt**
- **water**
- **small bucket**

STEPS

1. Find a flat surface near a low-hanging tree branch.

2. Arrange small rocks in two rows near the tree branch. Stack more rocks on top, continuing until you reach the desired size of your wall.

3. Tie one end of the rope to the branch and the other end to a large rock. The rock should hang at the same level as the center of the wall.

4. Put on the safety glasses or sunglasses. Pull back on the large rock and release, letting it smash into the rock wall. Observe the damage. If the rock wall is still intact, pull back the rock again at a different angle and release.

5. Using the stick, mix dirt and water in a bucket to form a thick mud.

6. Rebuild the wall by stacking the rocks in rows like in step 2. This time, apply the mud to the sides and tops of the rocks before placing them in the wall, and let the mud harden.

7. Try smashing the wall again. Do you notice a difference?

WHY? When mud is placed between layers of interlocking rocks and allowed to dry, it acts like glue, making the structure more durable. Cement and other reinforcing materials add a lot of strength to structures such as walls and buildings.

STEAM Connection: The Great Wall of China, which took centuries to complete, was constructed from stone, earth, and mortar consisting of lime, water, and— a very unusual material—sticky rice!

OBSERVATIONS: What happened as you made your wall taller without the mud? Which wall stood up best to the rock?

Try This! Change the shape of the wall to see if it affects its strength. Try making it curved, or make the base wider than the top.

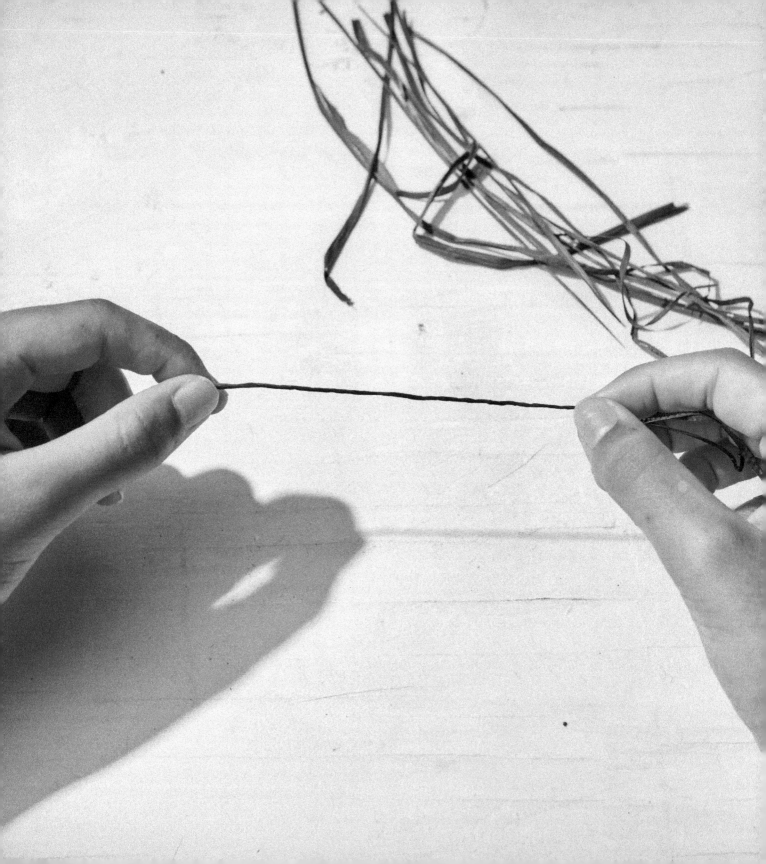

TWISTED PLANT ROPE

LEVEL: CHALLENGING

TIME: 15 MINUTES

REAL QUESTION

Can grass be made into rope?

MATERIALS

- **12 long blades of grass that are roughly the same size or 12 strips of plant material from cattails or other fibrous plants**

STEPS

1. Take 2 blades of grass and twist them together until the center forms a small loop, or kink.

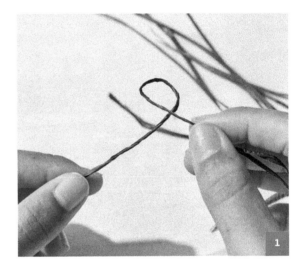

2. Hold the grass just below the loop with your nondominant hand and continue twisting the grass using the reverse wrap technique.

CONTINUED →

3. With your dominant hand, twist the strand on top away from you and then bring it forward and move the bottom strand to the top so that the strands switch places. This can be tricky and takes some practice!

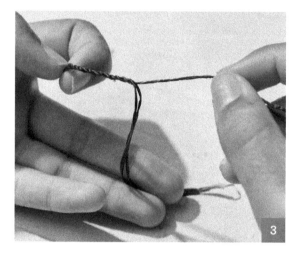

4. Repeat step 3.

5. Continue in this pattern of twisting away and bringing over, moving your nondominant hand down the strand for stability as you go.

6. Add more pieces of grass by twisting them in as you go. Place the new blades of grass just slightly above the ends you're twisting to ensure they won't slip out. You can trim off the ends that stick out later.

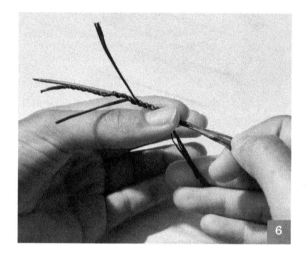

7. When you have reached the length of rope you want, simply tie a knot in the end of your grasses, joining all strands together. You have now made a rope out of plants!

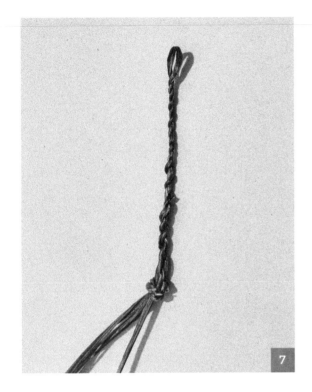

WHY? The reverse wrap causes the strands in your cordage to push against each other in opposite directions, creating **friction** that prevents them from unwinding. Ropes made without that twist will quickly unravel into separate strands.

STEAM Connection: Ropes made out of metal fibers are often used in elevators, cranes, and suspension bridges. Their structure of twisted strands makes them more durable and less prone to failure than metal chains.

OBSERVATIONS: How strong is your rope? Could you lift a bucket full of water with it?

Try This! Make two ropes and reverse wrap them together to make an even thicker rope!

Chapter Five

Experimenting with Energy and Force

In this chapter, we'll make things move! Applying a push or a pull to an object creates **force** that can launch seeds or even shoot off a rocket. But energy and force can also have surprising effects.

Are you brave enough to try dancing on liquid? Is it possible to pass a wire through a solid block of ice? Try these experiments and find out!

GRAVITY-DEFYING WATER

LEVEL: EASY

TIME: 5 MINUTES

REAL QUESTION

Can water stay in a cup when the cup is upside down?

MATERIALS

- cup
- water
- 2 flat pieces of cardboard or plastic

STEPS

1. Fill the cup halfway full of water and place 1 piece of cardboard or plastic across the top.

2. Place one hand firmly over the cardboard or plastic.

3. Carefully turn the cup upside down, then slowly remove the hand that is supporting the lid. Observe. Does the water stay in the cup? What happens if you shake the cup?

3

6. Slowly move your hand away from the lid. Does the water stay in the cup?

WHY? Air pressure is pushing on us all the time, but we don't usually notice because we're so used to it. The air pressure is what keeps the water in the cup. If there were a small hole in the cup, then the water would fall straight out.

> **STEAM Connection:** Machines that use compressed air, like jackhammers, are called **pneumatic** tools. They work by pushing a lot of air into a small space, which creates high pressure that is released to power the tool.

OBSERVATIONS: Did the water stay in the cup? What happened when you shook the cup?

> **Try This!** Use a rubber band to secure a piece of cheesecloth or mesh fabric over the cup. Does this keep the water in the cup?

4. Turn the cup right-side up and remove the lid. Fill the cup with water again, this time completely full.

5. Cover the cup of water. If using cardboard as a lid, get a fresh piece that is not wet. If using plastic, you can reuse the same piece as before. With one hand placed over the lid, turn the cup upside down.

PLOP AND SPLAT PAINTINGS

LEVEL: EASY

TIME: 10 MINUTES

REAL QUESTION

Will splat patterns be different at different heights?

MATERIALS

- rag or washcloth, cut into 4 pieces
- 4 rubber bands
- measuring cups
- 4 different colors Berry Good Ink (page 36) or craft paint
- water
- 4 small containers
- 4 pieces of paper or cardboard

STEPS

1. Make 4 cloth balls by crumpling each piece of rag or washcloth into a ball and then wrapping a rubber band around it.

2. Place ¼ cup of a different color of berry ink or paint into each of the containers and mix each with ¼ cup of water.

3. Set the paper on the ground so that the pieces overlap and create a large square.

4. Place 1 cloth ball into each container so that it absorbs some of the colored water.

5. When ready to make a splat, pick up one of the cloth balls. Hold the ball 1 foot above the paper and let it fall, creating a color pattern.

6. Dip the cloth ball in the colored water again. Repeat the drop but this time hold it as high as you can. Notice any differences in the shape of the splat.

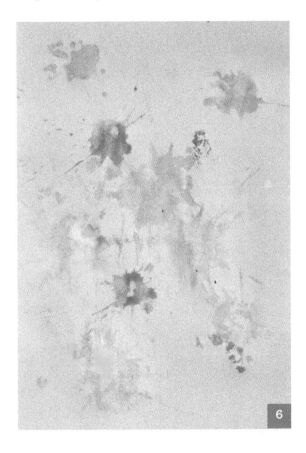

6

7. Repeat the process with the other colors. When you are done, set aside the painting to dry.

WHY? When the cloth ball hits the paper fast, the water inside the cloth is moving with a lot of energy. That energy, or **momentum**, pushes water out the surface of the cloth, creating a splatter mark on the paper. Wetter and faster cloth balls create the largest splats because they have more momentum. Momentum can be increased by either a larger mass (more water in the cloth) or a faster speed (faster drop).

STEAM Connection: Scientists can tell how fast a meteorite was traveling by studying the shape and size of an impact crater on Earth. Just like the fast-moving balls in this art project created bigger splats, larger and faster meteorites create bigger impact craters.

OBSERVATIONS: Did higher drops create bigger splats?

Try This! Tape the paper upright to a rock or a wall and throw the cloth balls to create a different type of splatter art.

DIRT TRACK DERBY

LEVEL: MEDIUM

TIME: 20 MINUTES

REAL QUESTION

What shape of ramp can move a ball between two points the fastest using gravity?

MATERIALS

- 10 cups sand or dirt that can be used to shape a track
- ruler
- water
- 2 or more marbles or Ping-Pong balls
- stopwatch (optional)

STEPS

1. Use the sand and the ruler to build a track that starts at least 5 inches above the finish line. Add water as needed so the sand holds its shape.

2. Build another track with the same start and finish elevations but with a steeper path in the middle. This should dip much lower than the first track.

CONTINUED →

3. Use your hand to smooth both tracks, making them as smooth as possible to minimize friction.

4. Place 1 marble at the top of each track and let go of them at the same time. Which track gets the marble to the finish line the fastest? If desired, time them using a stopwatch.

5. Repeat steps 1 through 4 with other track designs.

WHY? When a marble falls, its **potential energy** is converted into **kinetic energy**. The bigger the difference in height, the greater the speed the marble will have. This means that the shortest path to the finish line is not necessarily the fastest! A steeper drop near the start can provide enough speed to send a marble to the finish line first, even though it ends at the same elevation as the other marble.

STEAM Connection: Whether working with cars, cannons, or cranes, engineers face the challenge of effectively using gravity to accomplish a physical task. It can be difficult to account for friction using only math, so experimental design is often the best way to find the most efficient method of completing a goal.

OBSERVATIONS: Which track design was fastest? Did different balls perform better on different tracks?

Try This! Time the race with the marbles starting at the halfway point. Does it take half as long to finish? Come up with a hypothesis about why.

SHAPE-SHIFTING LIQUID

LEVEL: MEDIUM

TIME: 15 MINUTES

REAL QUESTION

Can a fluid be both a solid and a liquid at the same time?

MATERIALS

- tarp or garbage bag and rocks (optional)
- roasting pan or other container big enough to step in
- 6 cups cornstarch
- 3 cups water
- stick or wooden spoon

STEPS

1. Find a location that can get messy and be rinsed off with water. Alternatively, place a tarp or garbage bag on the ground and secure it with rocks in the corners. Place the roasting pan on the ground or in the center of the tarp.

2. Pour the cornstarch into the roasting pan. Add the water and use a stick to carefully mix together.

3. When stirring fast, the mixture will be stiff and crack like a solid. When stirring slowly, the mixture will behave like a liquid.

4. With bare feet, hop into the container and then immediately hop out. Observe the results.

WHY? Cornstarch and water form a **non-Newtonian fluid**, a type of fluid that changes **viscosity** (how it flows) based on the amount of pressure applied to it. Pressure causes the **polymer chains** of cornstarch to become intertwined, giving it a more solid consistency. When the pressure is released, the polymers flow past each other and the mixture behaves as a liquid.

STEAM Connection: Your body contains non-Newtonian fluids! Joints, such as your knees, contain synovial fluid, a lubricant that acts like a cushion to the joint and the cartilage surrounding it when a force is applied to the joint.

OBSERVATIONS: Which movements made your cornstarch mixture appear solid? Which made it appear liquid?

Try This! In smaller containers, experiment with different ingredients. Do cornstarch and oil create a non-Newtonian fluid? What about flour and water?

5. Dance on the cornstarch mixture. Observe the results.

6. Stand still in the mixture. Observe the results.

7. To clean up, let the cornstarch dry, then dispose of it in the trash or a compost pile, or use a hose to rinse away the cornstarch.

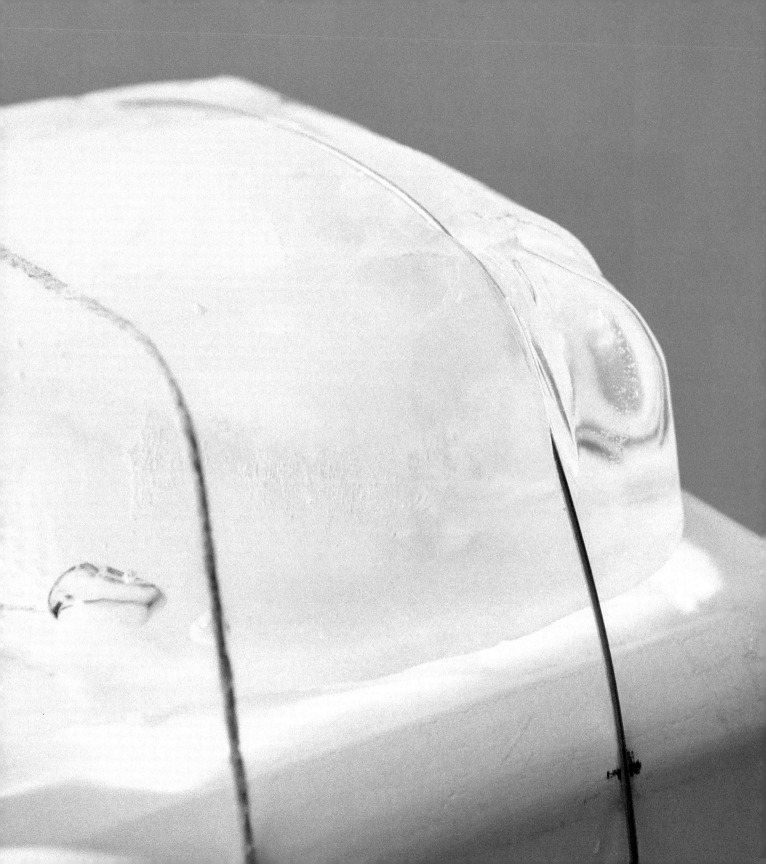

ICE SLICE

LEVEL: CHALLENGING

TIME: 2 HOURS, PLUS OVERNIGHT
TO FREEZE

REAL QUESTION

Can you cut through ice with pressure?

MATERIALS

- 1 (12-ounce or larger) food storage container
- water
- 4 equal weights, such as unopened water bottles or hand weights
- 1 (3-foot-long) piece of thin wire
- 1 (3-foot-long) piece of yarn
- wall or large rock that is elevated from the ground

STEPS

1. Fill the container with water and place it in the freezer overnight.

2. Tie 2 water bottles or weights to each end of the wire. Tie the other 2 bottles to each end of the yarn. You should have 2 "strings" with equal-size weights hanging from each end.

3. Find an elevated surface outside to place your ice block on, like the top of a wall or a large rock.

4. Remove the ice block from the container and place it on the elevated surface.

CONTINUED →

5. Drape the wire and yarn over the ice block so the weights hang evenly on either side of the ice.

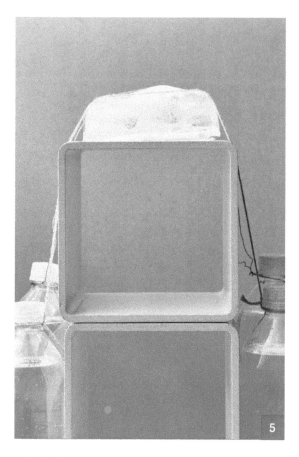

6. Check the ice block every 20 minutes to see which material is doing a better job of cutting through the ice.

WHY? Pressure can lower the melting point of ice, causing it to melt. Metal wire cuts ice better than yarn because it conducts heat. But given enough time, both can cut through ice if their pressure is great enough.

STEAM Connection: The process of ice melting under pressure and then refreezing is called **regelation**. This occurs naturally in glaciers and assists in a favorite wintertime activity—snowball fights! When you gather snow and squish it between your hands to form a ball, you cause some snow to melt. When you open your hands and release the pressure, the snow freezes again, binding the ball together.

OBSERVATIONS: Which material cut the ice better? What did you notice happening to the ice after the wire entered the block?

Try This! Repeat this experiment with a different amount of weight. Does more pressure cause faster regelation?

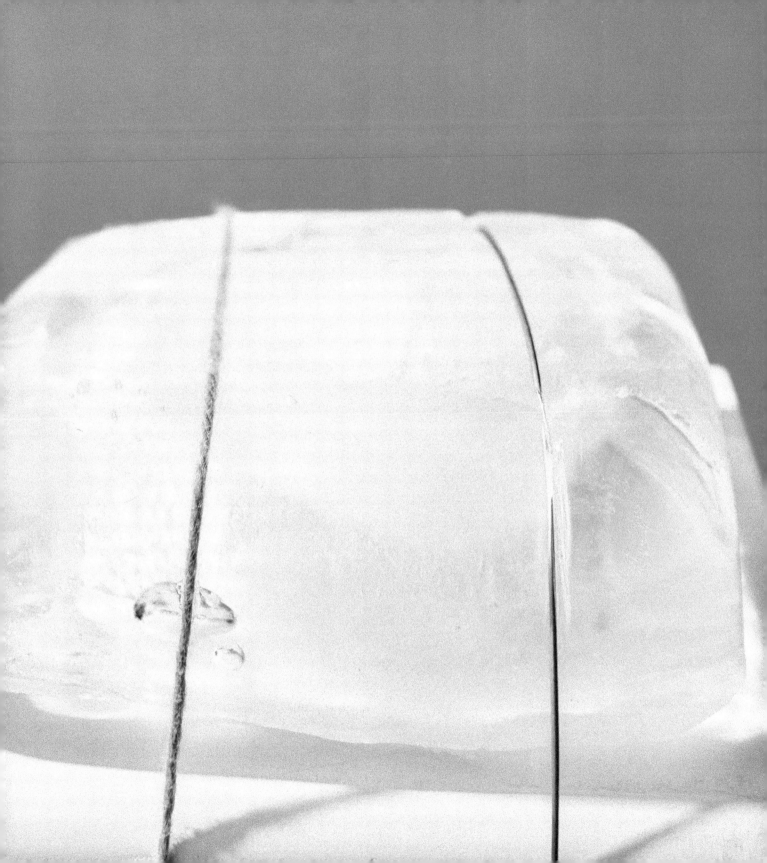

SUPER SEED SLINGS

LEVEL: CHALLENGING

TIME: 30 MINUTES

REAL QUESTION

Can we use physics to speed up planting seeds?

⚠ CAUTION: Eye protection is recommended for this experiment.

MATERIALS

- **large bowl**
- **¼ cup wildflower seeds native to your area**
- **1 cup dirt**
- **water**
- **spoon**
- **12 rubber bands**
- **1 (4-inch-square) piece of cloth with a small hole cut near each corner**
- **Y-shaped stick**
- **safety glasses or goggles**

STEPS

1. In a large bowl, mix together the seeds and dirt. Add water one spoonful at a time, mixing with your hands. Add just enough water to make the mixture damp.

2. Use your hands to shape the mud into Ping-Pong-size balls. These are the wildflower "seed bombs."

3. Place 1 rubber band through one of the holes near a corner of the cloth. Pull it through itself to form a simple knot with a loop. Loop another rubber band through the first one, then a third rubber band through the second, to create a rubber band rope extending from the cloth.

4. Repeat step 3 with each hole in the cloth.

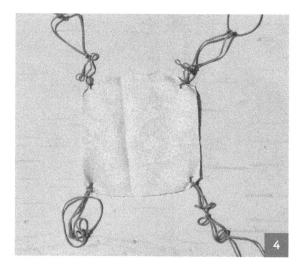

5. To make the slingshot, insert each top end of the *Y*-shaped stick through two of the rubber band ropes.

5

6. To launch the seed bombs, choose an area where wildflowers can grow. Always ask permission before launching seeds onto property that is not yours.

7. Put on the safety glasses. Then place a seed bomb in the cloth. Hold the base of the stick with one hand and pull back on the cloth with the other.

8. Aim the slingshot in the direction you want to send the seeds, then release the cloth. Try different angles and see which works the best.

WHY? As you pull on the rubber bands, you are storing potential energy. Releasing them converts the potential energy into kinetic energy.

STEAM Connection: Planting thousands of seeds by hand is time-consuming. Seed bombing can be much more effective. As seed bombs hit the ground, they break apart, scattering seeds over the surface.

OBSERVATIONS: Did the angle of the slingshot make a difference in how far the seeds traveled?

Try This! Scale it up and make a larger version.

BAKING SODA ROCKET

LEVEL: CHALLENGING

TIME: 30 MINUTES

REAL QUESTION

How do rockets fly?

! CAUTION: This experiment requires adult supervision and needs to be performed in a large open area with no overhead obstructions. Eye protection is recommended for this experiment.

MATERIALS

- bottle cork or piece of Styrofoam
- empty plastic bottle
- duct tape
- 3 (10-inch-long) sticks
- 1 tablespoon baking soda
- 1 (4-inch-square) piece of paper towel
- 1 (9-inch-long) piece of thread
- 1 cup vinegar
- safety glasses or goggles

STEPS

1. Stuff the cork into the bottle, making sure it fits snugly.

2. Flip the bottle upside down and use duct tape to attach the sticks around the sides of the bottle at equal intervals. The ends of the sticks should extend beyond the cork so the bottle is stable and freestanding when upside down.

3. Place the baking soda in the center of the paper towel square.

4. Fold the edges of the paper towel over the baking soda and tie it up with the thread. Make sure the baking soda packet will fit through the bottle opening and that at least

CONTINUED →

4 inches of thread will extend from the packet and out of the bottle. Set aside.

5. Remove the cork and pour the vinegar into the bottle.

6. Put on the safety glasses. Carefully insert the baking soda packet into the bottle, holding the string so the packet stays suspended above the vinegar. Push the cork tightly into the bottle so it holds the thread in place.

7. Flip the bottle over so it is standing on its stick legs, and back away. The liquid inside will start to foam and propel the rocket from the ground.

WHY? Newton's third law of motion says that for every action, there is an equal and opposite reaction. The downward force of gas leaving the bottle pushes the bottle upward, launching it into the air.

STEAM Connection: NASA's rockets depend on Newton's laws of motion, just like your rocket. A rocket engine produces exhaust gas, which is pushed through a nozzle to the back of the rocket.

OBSERVATIONS: How high did your rocket fly? Did it lift off almost immediately after being turned upside down?

Try This! Use cardboard, markers, and tape to decorate your rocket. You could add fins and a pointed nose to make it more aerodynamic. Or eyes and tentacles so it looks like a flying squid!

SAND ART PENDULUM

LEVEL: CHALLENGING

TIME: 30 MINUTES

REAL QUESTION

Does a pendulum always follow the same path?

CAUTION: Adult supervision is required when using power tools.

MATERIALS

- **large piece of cardboard or black paper**
- **low-hanging tree branch over a flat surface**
- **scissors**
- **empty plastic bottle**
- **drill or nail**
- **8 feet of twine or yarn, cut into 3 (1-foot-long) pieces and 1 (5-foot-long) piece**
- **sand or sugar (enough to fill the bottle)**

STEPS

1. Place the cardboard on a flat surface underneath a branch.

2. With an adult helper, use the scissors to cut the bottom ¼ inch off the bottle. Use the drill to make a small (⅛-inch) hole in the lid. Make sure the hole is big enough for the sand to flow through freely.

3. Have your adult helper drill three holes ½ inch from the bottom edge of the bottle and tie 1 (1-foot) piece of twine through each hole. Tie the three strands together.

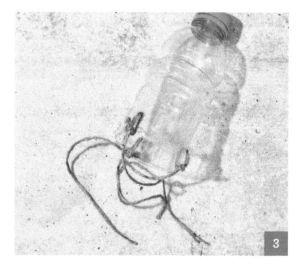

4. Tie the 5-foot piece of twine to the tree branch above the cardboard. If necessary, cut the twine so the end is above the ground.

5. Tie the long piece of twine to the three strands. The bottle should hang a few inches above the cardboard.

6. Fill the bottle with sand or sugar, pressing your finger over the hole in the lid so the sand or sugar doesn't fall out.

7. Pull the bottle back, remove your finger from the hole, and gently release the bottle. The direction you send the bottle will determine the pattern of the sand.

WHY? As you release the bottle and gravity pulls it down, the taut string causes the bottle to travel toward the position it would hang at rest. Any sideward force applied when releasing will cause the bottle to spiral. The bottle swings like a pendulum until air resistance and friction bring it to a stop.

STEAM Connection: Galileo showed that the time it takes for a pendulum to swing from one side to another (its period) depends only on the length of the string. This fact is used to create pendulum clocks. Today, geologists use pendulums in seismometers to detect earthquakes.

OBSERVATIONS: Did different angles create different patterns?

Try This! Tie a string to two points above the flat surface, then attach the main twine of the pendulum to create a *Y* shape. By varying the lengths of the *Y*-shape parts, you can create patterns known as Lissajous curves! Fill the bottle with layers of colored sand for an eye-catching work of art.

Chapter Six

Experimenting with Matter and Elements

Matter is anything that has mass and volume. **Physical reactions** don't change what the matter is. Water is still water whether it is frozen or liquid. In **chemical reactions**, matter does change! For example, when you mix vinegar with baking soda, you get carbon dioxide, a gas that wasn't there before.

This chapter will help you explore the elements through fun experiments like filtering Kool-Aid with dirt or melting ice without heat. You'll also make pop-proof balloons and even extract chlorophyll from leaves. In every activity, you'll see that chemistry is all around us.

control

SOIL PH TEST

LEVEL: EASY

TIME: 10 MINUTES

REAL QUESTION

How can you determine if soil is acidic or **alkaline**?

MATERIALS

- **3 paper cups or containers**
- **pencil**
- **tape**
- **1½ cups dirt**
- **1 cup water**
- **½ cup vinegar**
- **small bowl**
- **1 teaspoon baking soda**
- **spoon**

STEPS

1. Using the pencil and tape, label the containers. On one, write "control"; on the next, write "vinegar"; and on the last, write "baking soda."

2. Place ½ cup of dirt into each container. Remove any leaves, roots, or worms.

3. To the control container, add ½ cup of water. Observe for bubbles or fizzing.

CONTINUED →

4. To the vinegar container, add the vinegar. Observe for bubbles or fizzing.

5. In the small bowl, mix together the remaining ½ cup of water and 1 teaspoon of baking soda. Add the mixture to the container labeled "baking soda." Observe for bubbles or fizzing.

6. Record your observations. If you witnessed a reaction with the vinegar, your soil is alkaline (basic) and has a pH above 7. If you saw reactions with the baking soda, your soil is acidic and has a pH below 7. If all three cups looked the same and no reaction occurred, then your soil is considered neutral, with a pH of 7.

WHY? The pH, or "potential of hydrogen," determines whether something is an acid or a base. The more hydrogen ions something has, the more acidic it is. The fewer it has, the more basic it is. Vinegar will react with bases such as alkaline soil. Baking soda will react with acidic compounds such as acidic soil.

STEAM Connection: Farmers and gardeners need to know the pH level of their soil to prevent diseases and grow good crops. Certain plants, like blueberries, will grow only in acidic soil.

OBSERVATIONS: What reactions did you observe? Was your soil acidic, alkaline, or neutral?

Try This! After finishing the experiment, add the dirt with the vinegar to the baking soda container. What happens?

Soil pH in the Continental US

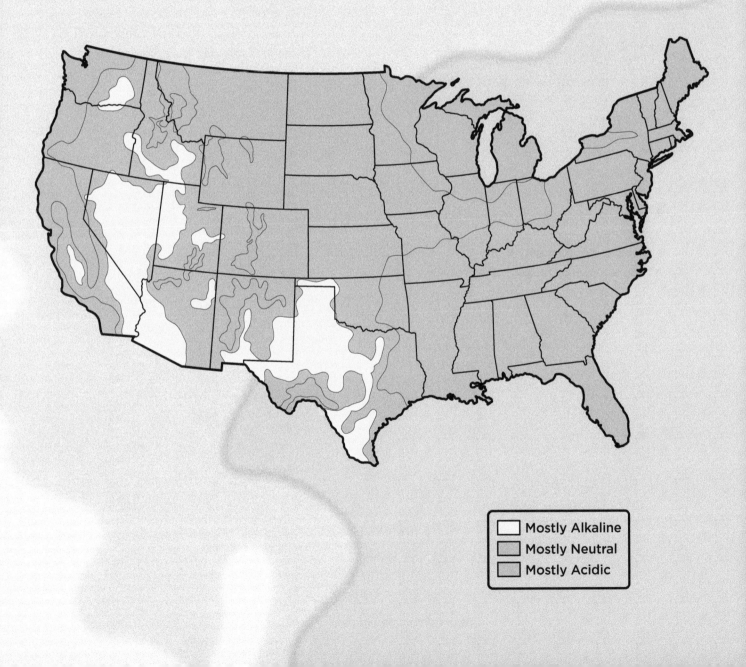

☐	Mostly Alkaline
▨	Mostly Neutral
▨	Mostly Acidic

MELTING MATCH

LEVEL: EASY

TIME: 10 TO 25 MINUTES, DEPENDING ON TEMPERATURE AND HUMIDITY

REAL QUESTION

Can ice be melted by factors other than heat?

MATERIALS

- **5 ice cubes**
- **small spoon**
- **sugar**
- **salt**
- **pepper**
- **sand or cocoa powder**
- **pen and paper for recording results**

STEPS

1. Line up the ice cubes where it is okay for them to melt. Be sure all the cubes have the same light exposure and temperature. For faster results, do this experiment on a warm day.

2. Leave 1 ice cube alone. This is the control.

3. Put a spoonful of sugar on the second ice cube.

4. Put a spoonful of salt on the third one. Put pepper on the fourth and sand on the fifth cube. If desired, use more ice cubes to test other substances for their melting ability.

5. Check on the ice cubes every couple of minutes, and use a pen and paper to record how much each has melted.

6. Continue recording the results until each cube is melted completely.

WHY? Salt water and sugar water both have lower freezing points than pure water, so salt and sugar will cause ice to melt faster. Ice cubes with pepper or sand on top will also melt faster than the control because darker colors absorb more heat than lighter colors.

STEAM Connection: In winter, roads are treated with salt to prevent cars from slipping on icy surfaces. The salt not only thaws the ice but also prevents it from refreezing because it changes the freezing point of the ice from 32°F to nearly 0°F. A road that has been salted will freeze and become icy only if air temperatures drop to match the new freezing point of 0°F.

OBSERVATIONS: Which material melted an ice cube most quickly?

Try This! Bury ice cubes in different materials, such as damp dirt, dry leaves, or grass. See which ice cube melts first!

SIZZLING SELTZER

LEVEL: EASY

TIME: 15 MINUTES

REAL QUESTION

Does temperature affect chemical reactions?

MATERIALS

- 2 jars or cups
- 1½ cups water
- snow or ice cubes
- microwave-safe mug
- pot holder
- 3 Alka-Seltzer tablets
- stopwatch or timer
- pen and paper

STEPS

1. Fill the jars with ½ cup of water each.

2. Place 1 cup in an environment that is room temperature. Place the other cup in snow. If you don't have snow, add ice to the second cup and remove some water so that the total volume is still ½ cup. Let it sit for about 10 minutes so the temperature of the water will change.

3. After 10 minutes, pour the remaining ½ cup of water into the microwave-safe mug and heat it in the microwave for 1 minute on high power.

4. Bring all 3 jars to the same area for observation, using the pot holder for the hot mug.

5. Drop 1 Alka-Seltzer tablet into each cup at the same time, and start the stopwatch.

6. Observe the reaction of the tablets. Use the pen and paper to record how long it takes for each tablet to dissolve.

WHY? A chemical reaction occurs when the Alka-Seltzer dissolves. Molecules of sodium bicarbonate and citric acid begin to collide, creating carbon dioxide, which is seen as bubbles. Higher temperatures cause molecules to move at faster speeds. This is why the chemical reaction happens faster in warm or hot water rather than cold.

STEAM Connection: Pharmacologists are medical scientists who use their knowledge of chemical reactions to research medications and how they are broken down and dispersed within the body. Many work to develop medicines for treatment of diseases, such as cancer.

OBSERVATIONS: Which temperature produced the quickest reaction? Which was the slowest?

Try This! Do a different version of this experiment: Fill two cups with ½ cup water each but keep the water temperature the same and test the difference between dropping in a whole Alka-Selzer tablet versus a crushed tablet. Does the tablet's surface area affect the reaction?

STICKY ICE CONTEST

LEVEL: EASY

TIME: 5 MINUTES

REAL QUESTION

Can you pick up an ice cube using only salt and a toothpick? How about using a string?

MATERIALS

- 4 ice cubes or, if it's winter, small pieces of ice found outside
- 2 toothpicks or straight sticks
- cup of water
- salt (finer-grain salt works better)
- 2 (5-inch-long) pieces of string or yarn

STEPS

1. Place 2 ice cubes on a flat surface.

2. Dip the toothpicks into the cup of water and lay one on top of each ice cube.

3. Sprinkle salt over one of the toothpicks. Let sit for 20 seconds. Then pick up both toothpicks without touching the ice cubes.

CONTINUED →

4. Set out 2 ice cubes and the pieces of string or yarn.

5. Dip the pieces of yarn in the cup of water and lay 1 piece over each ice cube.

6. Sprinkle salt over one of the yarn pieces. Let sit for 20 seconds. Then pick up both pieces of yarn without touching the ice cubes.

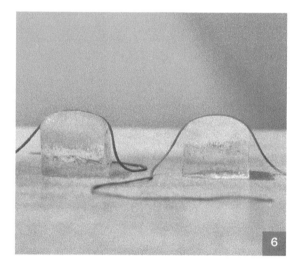

WHY? Liquid water has more energy than solid water. That means melting ice requires an *input* of energy! Ice melting next to a fire gets its energy from the fire's heat. Ice melting because of salt pulls energy directly from the nearest source, which is the ice itself! This temporarily makes the ice so cold that it freezes the salty water, sticking the ice to anything touching the salt!

STEAM Connection: Before freezers existed, people made ice cream using salt. The first ice cream was made by combining milk, flavoring, and flour, and then placing it in snow mixed with salt. The salt lowered the temperature of the snow, allowing it to freeze the milk mixture.

OBSERVATIONS: Were you able to lift both the salted and unsalted ice cubes? Were the ice cubes easier to lift using the toothpicks or yarn?

Try This! Materials other than salt can change the freezing point of water. Repeat this experiment using sugar or baking soda to see if you get the same results.

SURPRISING SOIL FILTERS

LEVEL: MEDIUM

TIME: 25 MINUTES

REAL QUESTION

Can soil filter water?

MATERIALS

- scissors
- 3 paper cups
- paper towel, cut into 3 pieces
- 1½ cups sand
- 1½ cups dirt
- 3 (1-pint) mason jars
- large jar or water pitcher
- 1 (0.13-ounce) package grape (purple) Kool-Aid or other drink mix that has artificial color
- 2 quarts water

STEPS

1. Carefully use the scissors to poke 10 small holes into the bottom of each paper cup.

2. Place 1 piece of paper towel in each cup so it covers the holes.

3. Add 1 cup of sand to the first cup. Add ½ cup of sand to the second cup and cover it with ½ cup of dirt. Add 1 cup of dirt to the third cup.

4. Create a small depression, or dip, in the top of the sand or dirt in each cup. Place a paper cup in each mason jar.

5. In a large jar, mix the Kool-Aid with the water. If using a different drink mix, make it according to the package directions.

6. Slowly pour ½ cup of Kool-Aid into the depression you made in the sand or dirt in each cup. Once the liquid has filtered through, slowly add another ½ cup of Kool-Aid.

7. Compare the color of the filtered liquid with the original purple color of the Kool-Aid.

WHY? Most soil particles have a negative charge. The amount of negative charge in the soil depends on the amount of silt, sand, and clay it contains. Positively charged particles in the Kool-Aid (such as the food dyes) bind to the clay particles in the soil.

STEAM Connection: Unlike water collected from rivers and lakes, groundwater is often clean and ready to drink because the soil holds on to pollutants, like bacteria, chemicals, and minerals, and lets clean water run through to collect in an **aquifer**.

OBSERVATIONS: Did any of the dirt-filled cups produce blue or clear water instead of purple?

Try This! Repeat this experiment using different colors from other food coloring, such as orange or green.

COLORFUL CHLOROPHYLL

LEVEL: CHALLENGING

TIME: 40 MINUTES

REAL QUESTION

Why are most leaves green?

⚠ CAUTION: Do not use leaves from poisonous plants, such as poison ivy. Be careful when handling hot water.

MATERIALS

- 5 dark green leaves
- 5 light green, yellow, or red leaves
- scissors
- 2 small heatproof cups
- spoon
- large heatproof bowl or pan
- rubbing alcohol
- microwave-safe mug
- water
- pot holders
- tape
- 2 (½-inch-wide) strips cut from a paper towel or coffee filter
- 2 pencils or sticks

STEPS

1. Collect the dark green and light green leaves. For best results, choose leaves that are soft and easily mashed.

2. Use the scissors to cut one type of leaf into small pieces. Place the cut-up leaves in 1 heatproof cup and mash with the spoon.

3. Repeat step 2 with the other type of leaf. Place both cups in the large heatproof bowl or pan.

4. Pour just enough rubbing alcohol into each cup to cover the leaves completely.

CONTINUED ➔

5. Fill the mug with water and microwave until very hot, about 2 minutes. Using the pot holders, carefully pour the cup of hot water into the bowl or pan, being sure to add the water *outside* of the cups.

6. Using the tape, secure 1 paper towel strip to the middle of each pencil. If you don't have tape, simply drape the paper towel strip over each pencil.

7. Lay the pencils across the cups so the strips touch the alcohol but not the sides of the cup.

8. Wait 20 minutes, then observe the paper towel strips. Do you see faint green lines at the top? That's chlorophyll!

WHY? Leaves are green because they contain a pigment called chlorophyll. But chlorophyll is not the only type of pigment in plants. Chlorophyll dissolves in alcohol, which is why you should see bands of pigment on the paper towel. Other pigments, like anthocyanins and **carotenoids**, have different-size particles, so they travel at different speeds up the paper towel.

STEAM Connection: Pigments are in many of your favorite foods! Carotenoids, such as beta-carotene, give cheese its orange color, and anthocyanins are responsible for the colors of many fruits and vegetables.

OBSERVATIONS: Did you see more than one color of pigment on the strip? Which leaf produced the most pigment?

Try This! Is chlorophyll in stems, too? Find green and brown plant stems and try the same extraction from them.

ORANGE is for carotenoids

GREEN is for chlorophyll

RED is for anthocyanin

YELLOW is for flavonoids

POP-PROOF BALLOONS

LEVEL: CHALLENGING

TIME: 15 MINUTES

REAL QUESTION

Can water keep balloons from popping?

> ⚠ **CAUTION:** This experiment involves focused heat from a magnifying glass. Never concentrate this heat on another person or creature or on dry material that could catch fire. Adult supervision and assistance are suggested.

MATERIALS

- **8 balloons (water balloons, latex balloons, or a combination)**
- **water**
- **sunglasses**
- **magnifying glass**

STEPS

1. On a sunny day, inflate 4 balloons with air. Tie them off and set aside. Ask an adult for help if you have trouble tying the balloons.

2. Fill 4 balloons with water. For best results, fill them completely. Tie them off and set aside.

3. Put on the sunglasses. (When using the magnifying glass, you should wear sunglasses because the spot of light can be very bright.) In a sunny area, place one of the air-filled balloons on the ground. If there is wind, have another person hold the balloon so it doesn't blow away.

4. Using the magnifying glass, focus the sun's rays so they make a very small spot of light on the balloon's surface. Does the balloon pop?

5. Now place the water-filled balloons on the ground and focus the light on one of them. Be patient, and keep the light focused. What happens?

6. Repeat steps 3 through 5 with the remaining balloons. Do you observe the same results?

WHY? A magnifying glass can focus heat and light on a very small point. It doesn't take much heat from the magnifying glass to pop an air-filled balloon. But a balloon filled with water is different. The water absorbs the heat until the focused light burns a hole in the rubber. Then, most often, a small stream of water emerges from the hole!

STEAM Connection: One reason firefighters use water to fight fires is due to its high **heat capacity.** The water absorbs a lot of heat from the fire as it changes into steam. If the temperature drops below the ignition temperature, the fire goes out.

OBSERVATIONS: Did both the air-filled and water-filled balloons pop? Which balloon popped more quickly?

Try This! Repeat this experiment with different amounts of water in the balloons. What happens to a balloon only half full of water?

Chapter Seven

Putting It All Together

Congratulations on completing these outdoor science experiments! You now have a greater understanding of how science, technology, engineering, art, and math are connected to, and influenced by, the great outdoors.

In chapter 3, you learned how nature relates to STEAM and all areas of science. Using the scientific method, you studied the intelligence of birds, how the amount of light affects photosynthesis and leaf development, and how sinkholes are formed. In chapter 4, you made tools from materials found outside and around your house to determine direction and to cook food with the sun. In chapter 5, you explored the concepts of force and energy, which shape our universe. This gave you a better understanding of Newton's third law of motion, the concepts of potential and kinetic energy, and non-Newtonian fluids. In chapter 6, you performed experiments to understand matter and elements, and how matter can change with or without a chemical reaction.

Experiencing the natural world through STEAM activities is a fun way to become familiar with the scientific method, which will help you in all your intellectual adventures. In nature, there are unlimited opportunities to:

- Explore a question

- Form a hypothesis

- Test the hypothesis

- Collect and analyze data

- Draw conclusions about the hypothesis

- Consider future research

The experiments in this book were designed to enhance your problem-solving and critical thinking skills as you learn more about the natural world and make exciting discoveries. Now it is time to launch your knowledge and enthusiasm into the world to create and test your own hypotheses: 3 . . . 2 . . . 1 . . . *blastoff*!

REAL OUTDOOR SCIENCE EXPERIMENTS

GLOSSARY

acidic: [uh-SI-dic] An acidic substance has more hydrogen ions (H+) than hydroxide ions (OH–), and has a pH less than 7

albedo: [al-BEE-doh] A measure of the amount of light reflected back from an object

alkaline (basic): [AL-kuh-line] An alkaline substance has more hydroxide ions (OH–) than hydrogen ions (H+), and has a pH greater than 7

anthocyanin: [an-tho-SAI-uh-nin] Water-soluble pigment found in many plants, which can be black, blue, red, or violet

aquifer: [AH-qui-fur] Underground layer of rock or soil that contains water

biomimicry: [BY-OH-mim-ih-kree] The imitation of living things in human-made structures, systems, or materials

carotenoid: [ka-RAH-tuh-noid] Fat-soluble pigments found in many types of plants that have a yellow or orange color

chemical reaction: [KEH-mi-kul ree-AK-shun] During a chemical reaction, the bonds between atoms change, resulting in the formation of new molecules

chlorophyll: [KLOR-uh-fil] A green pigment in plants, algae, and cyanobacteria that allows for the absorption of light to convert it to energy

compost: [COM-post] Decayed organic matter used as plant fertilizer is compost

decomposition: [dee-com-po-ZI-shun] The process of being broken down into microscopic pieces after an organism dies

durable: [DUR-a-bull] Able to withstand pressure or damage

element: [EL-i-ment] A substance made of a single type of atom and that cannot be broken down into different substances

energy: [EN-er-jee] The ability to do work

equinox: [EE-kwi-nox] When the sun is directly over the equator, which happens twice a year, once in spring (around March 20) and once in fall (around September 22)

fibrous: [FAI-bruhs] Containing fibers

force: [FORS] A push or a pull on an object

friction: [FRIK-shun] The force resisting motion when objects rub against each other, whose types include static, sliding, rolling, and fluid

germinate/germination: [JUR-mah-nate] The process by which a seed or spore begins to grow

gnomon curve: [NO-mawn KURV] A line that connects all the endpoints of shadows from the gnomon (the part of a sundial that casts a shadow throughout the day)

heat capacity: [HEET kuh-PA-si-tee] The amount of heat needed to raise the temperature of a body by 1 degree

hypothesis: [hai-PAW-thuh-sis] An educated guess involving two or more variables

invertebrate: [in-VER-ti-brut] Animals without a skeleton inside their bodies, such as insects, worms, snails, octopus, and jellyfish

kinetic energy: [ki-NEH-tic EN-er-jee] Energy due to motion

latitude: [LAT-i-tude] The distance of a place north or south from the equator

matter: [MA-ter] Anything that has mass in the form of either a solid, liquid, or gas and that takes up space

momentum: [moe-MEN-tum] The force or energy of a moving object, calculated by multiplying an object's size and speed

non-Newtonian fluid: [nawn-noo-TOH-nee-un FLOO-id] A fluid whose viscosity changes under force

organic matter: [or-GA-nik MA-ter] A carbon-based compound found in nature

pH: [pee-ACH] For "potential of hydrogen," a scale that measures whether an object is acidic or alkaline

photosynthesis: [foh-toh-SIN-thuh-sis] The process by which plants convert light energy from the sun, carbon dioxide, and water into food for the plant as well as oxygen

physical reaction: [FIH-zi-kul ree-AK-shun] During a physical reaction, a substance changes state but no new molecules are formed

pigment: [PIG-ment] A substance that produces color

pneumatic: [new-MAT-ic] Describes something, usually tools, that use or are powered by compressed air

polymer chain: [PAW-li-mer chayn] Small molecules, called monomers, that bond together chemically to form polymers

potential energy: [puh-TEN-shul EN-er-jee] An object's stored energy

regelation: [ree-juh-LAY-shun] The process by which ice melts with pressure, then refreezes once the pressure is removed

scientific method: [sai-un-TI-fick MEH-thud] A way of solving problems in which a hypothesis is made and tested, data are collected, and a conclusion based on evidence is presented

solstice: [SOL-stis] The time of year when the Earth is tilted to produce either the longest or shortest day of the year, typically June 21 and December 21

stomata: [STOW-mah-tah] These are small pores on plant leaves and stems that allow carbon dioxide to enter for use in photosynthesis and oxygen to be released

symmetry: [SIM-i-tree] When an object has similar parts that face each other and mathematically when it can be moved to a new orientation or position without changing its appearance

variable: [VAIR-ee-uh-bull] A condition that can change: it can be independent, something you change during the experiment; dependent, something that changes due to the independent variable; or controlled, something you keep the same for all conditions of the experiment

vermicompost: [VUR-mih-COM-post] A process of composting that uses worms to digest organic material and convert it to nutrients that are beneficial to plants

viscosity: [vis-KA-si-tee] How fast or slowly a liquid flows

RESOURCES

ADDITIONAL ACTIVITY BOOKS

Awesome Outdoor Science Experiments for Kids: 50+ STEAM Projects and Why They Work by Dr. Megan Olivia Hall (Rockridge Press)

Real Engineering Experiments: 25+ Exciting STEAM Activities for Kids by Anthony Tegtmeyer (Rockridge Press)

Real Science Experiments: 40 Exciting STEAM Activities for Kids by Jessica Harris (Rockridge Press)

BIRD IDENTIFICATION

Audubon website and app
Audubon.org/birding/identifying-birds

Merlin Bird ID
Merlin.AllAboutBirds.org

PLANT IDENTIFICATION

Seek app by iNaturalist
iNaturalist.org/pages/seek_app

U.S. Department of Agriculture PLANTS database
Plants.sc.egov.usda.gov/home

Virginia Tech weed identification
WeedID.cals.vt.edu

SCIENCE ACTIVITIES

NASA STEM Engagement
NASA.gov/stem/foreducators/k-12/index.html

Science Buddies
ScienceBuddies.org

INDEX

ACKNOWLEDGMENTS

A big thank-you to our patrons for testing experiments and answering surveys! Thank you to both Science Mom Amber and Science Mom Liza for your honest feedback and humor. Special thanks to Annie Choi and Mary Cassells for their excellent editorial advice and to Evi Abeler for the beautiful photos. Most of all, thank you, Math Dad, for tolerating many messes and keeping things running at home while I was busy experimenting and writing.

ABOUT THE AUTHOR

 **Jenny Ballif**, also known as Science Mom, has worked as a molecular biologist and a wildland firefighter and at several jobs that land in between wearing a lab coat and wielding a chainsaw. In 2013, she volunteered to bring weekly science experiments to her son's second-grade class, and her name changed from "Andrew's Mom" to "Science Mom." She's been sharing science with kids ever since. She and her partner, Math Dad, run the Science Mom YouTube channel. You can find their science videos and courses at Science.mom.

Printed in the USA
CPSIA information can be obtained
at www.ICGtesting.com
CBHW081244200224
4500CB00005B/21